POTENTIAL

† DON'T TAKE IT TO THE GRAVE †

Published by Godzchild Publications
a division of Godzchild, Inc.
22 Halleck St., Newark, NJ 07104
www.godzchildproductions.net

Printed in the United States of America 2013—First Edition
Cover design by Ana Saunders of Es3lla Designs

Library of Congress Cataloging-in-Publications Data
Potential: Don't Take It To the Grave/E.D. Richardson

ISBN 978-1-937095-70-3 (pbk).

1.Richardson, E.D. 2. Personal Growth 3. Potential
4. Spiritual Growth 5. Christianity

Unless otherwise indicated, Scripture quotations are taken from the King James Version (KJV), New International Version (NIV), and Amplified Version. All rights reserved.

TABLE OF CONTENTS

This book is segmented into five (5) divisions. Each division is of great necessity in order for you to live as God has created life to be, and for you to have the joy, peace, happiness, and fulfillment that may be currently missing. It is written to inform, encourage, and enlighten you so that you can live your life releasing your full potential.

It is my delight to dedicate this book to my deceased wife, Mary J. Richardson. She was a woman who demonstrated a life of divine purpose. Her last years on this earth were a clear example of getting the most out of what you have. Her health waned, and her struggles from day to day were very trying (to say the least). Yet she did not complain, and her mind was constantly on how she could help others, or be a blessing to the Kingdom of God. What a woman! So I thought it fit and proper to dedicate this book to her, as she did demonstrate much of what this book is about. I don't believe she took her potential to the grave! I believe that she served her God, her family, and others to her fullest ability. She left a legacy behind that lives on through the work she did, and the willingness to help others achieve their **_potential_**. So I release the information within with her in mind, that it could have been stated at her gravesite: "HERE LIES A WOMAN THAT RELEASED HER POTENTIAL." I trust that you will not only enjoy the contents herein, but that you will yield to the advice and receive the encouragement. May your life never be the same again!

PREFACE

A fter a few years of talking about it, the time finally came for me to pen these words so that many others can glean. I have experienced over the years of my life that a vast majority of people are not living out their *God-given purpose* on a daily, or even on a periodical basis. In fact, many do not know what they should or shouldn't be doing in life. Much of what we see is a *misplaced life* that is functioning in a wrong setting. Simply put, many people are not where they are supposed to be, and they are not doing what they are supposed to be doing! This is one of the reasons, if not the main reason that many people are so disgruntled with their lives. How often have you, or someone working with you complained about your job, finances, family matters, or your very own life? Much of what you hear is the reality of a *displaced life*! A displaced life is never positioned to live a fulfilled life!

My goal in writing this book is to open the eyes of your understanding, and to enlighten you by exposing the truth of where you are in life right now, versus where you should be. I am writing to distinguish *mere existence on earth from living your life to the fullest on this earth!* I believe you were created for *MORE! Do not take your potential to be more, have more, and bless others more to your grave.* Now it's time for you to believe in yourself again!

DIVISION I

Understanding Your Created Purpose

NOTES

———————————————— ❧ ————————————————

I t is because of the fall of mankind as a result of dis-
obedience to God, that we have a world that repre-
sents a distorted image of their Creator. If you do not
know, or realize what you are supposed to look like, act
like, or live like, then you obviously do not know what
or who you should be like. In order to have a clear and
decisive knowledge of who you are and what you should
be, you have to go back to your
spiritual DNA. It is according to
scientists that your DNA com-
position determines your char-
acteristic makeup. Your DNA,
therefore, has much to do with
your actions and what will or will
not happen to you as you age.
Armed with this information, it
is important that I look further back on the formation
of my life, beyond my natural parents. *Where did I come
from? How did I get here?* The only TRUTH that I have
for these questions is biblically based.

In Genesis 2:27 it declares: *"so God created man*

IF YOU DO NOT
KNOW, OR REAL-
IZE WHAT YOU ARE
SUPPOSED TO LOOK
LIKE, ACT LIKE, OR
LIVE LIKE, THEN
YOU OBVIOUSLY
DO NOT KNOW
WHAT OR WHO YOU
SHOULD BE LIKE.

in his own image, in the image of God created he him; male and female created he them." This scripture raises a lot of curiosity and concern about what my image is supposed to be, and what, or rather who should I represent while on this earth. *Why did God create me (man)? The following verse (28) gives some insight. It says: "and God blessed them, and God said unto them, BE FRUIT-FUL, and MULTIPLY, and replenish the earth, and subdue it: and have dominion over the fish of the sea and over the fowl of the air, and over every living thing that moveth upon the earth."*

It is in the words *fruitful* and *multiply* that I began to see a great deal of purpose for being here. But I discovered more, because my image of my creator was still something that was vital to my purpose. The Hebrew meaning (from which the old testament is translated) of *image* is *resemblance, a representative figure.* This means that I am to live in the earth realm for an allotted time, not representing myself, but resembling my Creator! As I researched the Holy Scriptures, I saw where man disobeyed God, and as a result, we became *spiritually disconnected.* It was that disconnect that caused the *natural and physical* man to seek self-satisfaction. And self-gratification has always brought about discontentment as an end result. So as the world continued to evolve and as we became more pronounced and civilized, man became more discontent and distorted in his Creator's image. Purposeful living became more and more unrealized from generation to generation. Today, we have a generation that is so distorted, so vain, so self-willed, and so disillusioned while attempting to find real peace and true fulfillment. It is only through understanding who created you and why, that man will begin to release that which God has placed him in the earth for.

As I looked a little further into my created purpose, I saw where I was created by God according to Isaiah 43:7 "for his glory." Glory in this text simply means to *honor.* So I was created to honor God. For real purpose to be carried out in my life, I must live to bring honor to God. *Hold on, I'm going to bring all of this together shortly!* I am now starting to understand why I was created. The life I experience now, is short, and will soon return to its Maker. The question I need to clarify in my mind, is, *"did I live this life to the fullest of my God-given abilities?"* If not, I go to my grave with potential that was never released! And that *potential* could have honored God in many ways, as well as made my *spiritual distorted image* much clearer. Not to mention, I also would have been much happier and contented with my life. So, having considered all of this, let me tie this together to bring understanding to you about your *created purpose.*

There are three distinct reasons for your creation. Those reasons are: _TO BE FRUITFUL, TO MULTIPLY,_ and _TO HONOR._ Let me deal with the first two. Fruitful and multiply are similar in definition, yet multiply carries a far greater revelation. Fruitful means *to bear, to bring forth, to grow, and to increase.*

WHEN YOU FAIL TO BEAR FRUIT IN YOUR LIFE, YOU FAIL TO GROW. AND WHEN YOU FAIL TO GROW, YOU FAIL TO INCREASE.

If your life is not in a mode of constant increase or productivity, then you fail to fully represent your Creator. Also, what you produce should bring satisfaction to you and bring a blessing to others. When you fail to bear fruit in your life, you fail to grow. And when you fail to grow, you fail to increase. And when you fail to increase, you will always find yourself unhappy with your life. The spirit of complaint will consume you. This is the emotional state of so many people. How often have you or someone with whom you've worked lived in a constant realm of dissatisfaction as a result of being unfruitful? Unfruitfulness literally means that you are _not releasing the purposeful abilities within you, in the purposed place of life._ Here is the message from this: *"what you do outside of purpose will never release as much potential as when you live in purpose!"* How many times has the question surfaced in your mind: "what am I here for?" How often is it, that deep within, you find yourself questioning your life and what it is producing? When you are uncertain of why you are on this earth, and when you are not conscious of the time you have on this earth, then you are prone to never release the potential within you.

To *multiply* is to do what the God of creation put you in the earth to do! To multiply means to *be full of, to make use of many times over, to enlarge and to excel, to nourish and to be plentiful in the process of time.* WOW! Here it is! God said that he created you to take the talents, gifts, and abilities that he placed in you, and nourish them and make full use of them. He said that you are to excel in your life, and to enlarge your reach to be a blessing to others. Your created purpose is produced from what you have multiplied many times over in the process of the time that he has allotted you on this earth! Now this is some powerful stuff right here! I would love for you to pause, take a deep breath, and profess out loud: "I WILL PRODUCE MANY TIMES OVER MY TALENTS, GIFTS, AND ABILITIES BEFORE I DIE!" AND YOU SHALL! There is more in you, there is more to you, and there is more that shall come from you! Why? Because you are now beginning to understand your created purpose. And as a result, you are becoming more motivated to arise from that place of unfruitfulness and implement the necessary changes that will propel you into your next dimension of living! YOU WERE CREATED FOR MORE! Knowing now that regardless of how you arrived on this planet, or what has transpired in your life in the past, you still have the opportunity to shine in this life like never before. Whether you are a believer in Jesus Christ or not, there is still more to your life on this earth than what you have experienced. It is better if you are a believer, because you have been spiritually reconnected. That also makes you sensitive to what it is that He has given you to do. You are special to God, and it is HIS desire that you utilize and maximize the talents and gifts that HE placed within you! There has to be a desire in you to exit out of the way it is now, and to enter into the way it was meant for you to be. Wherever you are in life right now, or whatever you may be doing, it is imperative that you take inventory of yourself and see if you are: a). HAPPY....b). CONTENT...and c). FULFILLED. These internal feelings are usually the result of exercising your life in the third created purpose that I mentioned earlier, and that is:

"for his glory." Or as also noted, to bring honor. This carries the connotation of living your life in the way that your creator purposed and equipped you to live, so that HE is satisfied with what you do.

In the book of Psalms, chapter 139:14…it says: *"I will praise thee, for I am fearfully and wonderfully made; marvelous are thy works, and that my soul knoweth right well."* God made you to be more, and to do more than what you may have already accomplished! There is no question that you were made to make a difference and to show a difference in your life. You know, if you are unhappy, discontent, and feeling unfulfilled, just think what God must be feeling about you. How can you bring him honor if you are not allowing what He equipped you with to be maximized? God is honored most when your talents and gifts are being used to yield increase. Something to think about! Does what you do respect God? Is the life you are living overwhelming you? Are others being blessed by what you do? Your answer must be "yes" in all three areas before you can honestly say that you are living in your created purpose and that you have tapped into your full potential. I am convinced that most of the world's population is out of place in what they were truly created to do. Again, allow me to echo something that was previously noted—there are too many disgruntled, unhappy, dissatisfied people doing something everyday that they hate or dislike! (This does not mean that someone is not helped or aided by what they are doing, but it does mean that they may still be out of THEIR purposed place). Thus, they live continuously feeling that there is something more that they can do, or something else that they should be doing. This is known as unfulfilled living! They are not overwhelmed with enjoyment and blessings; therefore, they are not being a blessing to others.

THERE IS NO QUESTION THAT YOU WERE MADE TO MAKE A DIFFERENCE AND TO SHOW A DIFFERENCE IN YOUR LIFE.

Are you reading this book and saying to yourself, *this man is talking about me?* If so, you did not come across this book by accident! God has designed a divine appointment for you and I to meet this way. There is still time for you to *shift* your life and enter into another *space* where your talents and gifts can flourish! Because you are reading this book, you still have time to make that change in order to be *fruitful*, *multiply*, and *honor God*.

Your Potential

Wat is potential? According to Webster's New Collegiate Dictionary, it means: *existing in possibility, and capable of development into actuality.* WOW! WOW! WOW! Based upon this definition, it is clear that all humans with potential have a possibility that has not yet been discovered! Within you is the God-given ability to do what once seemed impossible! I believe that you were created for more! But it is not enough for me to believe it, you must also believe it for yourself! What is it that you have a desire to do, yearn to do, and have not yet done? What is it that you know you probably should do, but have not acted on? Untapped potential lies within you, and it is up to you to tap into it and release it from within. It is like an undiscovered oil well that is filled with substance that can benefit many. How long will this precious gift, talent, and amazing ability go undiscovered? At what point, and what place in time will you arise and act on your potential? You can do it! You are more than what someone may have told you, or where you have found yourself in life. There is a new career, a new business, a new job, a new life, and a new beginning waiting on you! Get up, get focused, and move in the direction that was ordained by God for you before the foundation of the world.

As long as you are alive, it is never too late to make those necessary changes. Even if you feel that you *are where you should be, and you are doing what you should be doing; the questions become, are you maximizing your gifts? Are you bringing forth all that you are capable of producing? Is there more in you that can be released?* If the answers are no, no, and yes; then your potential has not yet been tapped into! You have more than you have been willing to yield. Have you paused long enough to ask yourself, *why haven't I given more or done more?* Usually, there are some underlying circumstances that are impeding your will to yield. Some of which I will address later in this book. But for now, the only real cause may be that you just haven't discovered a reason to maximize your talents, gifts, and abilities.

Selfishness is one of the greatest underlying causes for this. When the spirit of selfishness is in operation, a person is never willing to do any more than what is required to get by. They find themselves in a battle with themselves. They think that if they do more, it will only benefit another. But allow me to reiterate—you were created by God to honor, to multiply, and to bear fruit. God was not selfish in doing for you what He did, so it would be a blatant dishonor and disservice for you to think and act this way. Never feel that your best is only a benefit to others. Wherein others are to benefit from what you do in life, it is not secluded to them only. You are always the primary beneficiary of what you do. Your job, career, ministry, etc., is to bless you first. If you are not benefitting first, it literally be-comes impossible for anyone else to benefit. Do not allow the spirit of self-ishness to operate in you any longer. Dismiss it from your presence! Maxi-mize your talents! Maximize your gifts! Maximize your abilities! You have divine potential inside of you! God put it there when you were conceived, and it does not matter what you may have gone through in this life, it is still there. Move into the place in which you are sup-posed to function, and know that the only impossibility is what you haven't acted on. It is impossible to produce anything that you fail to act on. The grave is full of mil-lions upon millions of people who failed to act on what they were created to do. And it is full of people who died unfulfilled, unhappy, and dissatisfied all because they

> NEVER FEEL THAT YOUR BEST IS ONLY A BENEFIT TO OTHERS.

did not tap into their God-given potential.

When the subject of potential is discussed, there are many questions that arise; questions like: "How many people left this world who could have been doctors, lawyers, producers, publishers, actors/actresses, business owners, rocket scientists, world renowned authors, inventors, medical scientists, or engineers?" Yet, grave yards are full of never discovered potential! Will you become another statistic? Or will you lay aside the selfish spirit and step into a new life of discovering what it is that you were created to do and be? I, myself, built ships for twenty-two years before I discovered what I was truly created to do. I answered the call of God to become a Minister of the Holy Scriptures to the people that would hear. I made the decision to walk away from a secure job with medical benefits and a retirement plan (though at the time it was nothing great) in order to enter a whole new world and life that would allow me to maximize what God had put in me. This was naturally frightening. I had a family with small children at the time. I had debt and daily needs for a steady income; yet, I stepped away from a structured life and chose to trust God for provision. I founded a Church and the membership at the time was a staggering thirty. I share this with you to say this: if you are ever going to release the potential within you, *you have to step out into waters that you have never been in before.* This is often known as uncharted territory. Everything was new to me! This was a defining moment in my life! I had to first trust God's word for my life. My faith had to be in what He had promised me in His word. And one of the things that He promised me was that: *"lo, I am with you always, even unto the end of the world"* (Matthew 28:20b). I had to have the assurance that the Lord would be with me in my new adventure. I want you to have that same assurance. Another promise was that: *"and why take ye thought for raiment? Consider the lilies of the field, how they grow, they toil not, neither do they spin: and yet I say unto you, that even Solomon in all his glory was not arrayed like one of these. Wherefore, if God so clothed the grass of the field, which today is, and tomorrow is cast into the oven, shall he not much more clothe you, oh ye of little faith?"* (Matthew 6:28-30). When Jesus said this, he was delivering what is most popularly known as the Sermon-on-the-Mount. In the same way that Jesus assured them, He made it clear that he would take care of me if I would trust him. So I had to step out, so that I could step into! My entire life and future was on the line! I did not want to destroy the lives of my wife or children, or cause them to not believe in me as the leader of the family.

Prior to me making this move, I had become so unhappy and dissatisfied with my life. Going to work everyday had gone from a complete pleasure to a complete bore. I would literally dread getting up in the morning to go to work. I never had a problem with supporting and providing for my family, but I was having a difficult time at this point with what I was doing. I did not know back then what I know now. The problem that I was experiencing was not the job itself, but the untapped potential in me that was aching to get out. I was not functioning in my God created purpose. Emptiness and fruitlessness began to haunt me. It wasn't until I left that job and entered into this new arena of ministry that I, for the first time in my life, became really excited about getting up everyday and going to work. There was an inner peace that is hard to describe! There was happiness and joy that was now exuding from my life! I had momentarily taken a reduced salary, yet my family did not lack in supply or support. God provided! I discovered God's word to be true in my life! If I had

IT WASN'T UNTIL I EXITED THAT JOB AND ENTERED INTO THIS NEW ARENA OF MINISTRY WORK FULL TIME THAT I, FOR THE FIRST TIME IN MY LIFE, WAS REALLY EXCITED ABOUT GETTING UP EVERYDAY AND GOING TO WORK!

never walked away from what was a mere means of survival, and stepped into my God-given purpose, I would not be able to write this book that will bless millions of people. I would not have grown a fruitful ministry that is blessing people around the world today. I would not have established outreach works that are impacting my community in a positive way and many more. What I am currently releasing from my life would have never happened if I had stayed in mediocrity. Mediocrity is a "DREAM STEALER" and a "POTENTIAL KILLER," and should not be tolerated! Just like me, you have the ability to be exceptional and extraordinary! Understand that everyone, no matter how much you try to help, will not release their God-given potential. Everyone will not become an extraordinary individual. But then again, everyone is not reading this book either; YOU are! So, you must declare to yourself, "I am more than normal." You must do what the normal group of people will not if you are going to maximize and utilize your talents, gifts, and abilities. If you don't, your potential will go with your bones to the grave!

It is a proven fact, that *extraordinary* people do everyday what mediocre people never do, or only experiment with. Until there is a resolve within your spirit concerning your potential and your future, you will stay in the same place doing the same thing. It is true that the status-quo will stay uninspired and unchanged. I am telling you that God did not intend, from the beginning of man's creation, for us to be just a status-quo. You have so much more to draw from and to release from your life than what you see now. Your brain and your spirit has the ability to release more from it; when the two are in harmony with God's will, there is nothing that is impossible for you. Transformation takes place when your will to transition sanctions increase in your life. Potential is manifested and your life takes on a whole new meaning! One of the most exciting and amazing things that can happen to you is to know that you are maximizing your potential. Because you took the initiative to move out, to move away, and to move into your God created place in life, you will experience everything in a new light. There is a shift that takes place that brings to your life new associates, and ushers you into a new environment. Potential is released and fulfillment is felt. Enthusiasm surfaces and creative purpose is released. *Multiplication* and *increase* is seen, and honor should become evident to you.

As I shared earlier, when I stepped away from my full-time job, and stepped into my purpose, I began to multiply and increase. My life began to honor my Creator in a way that had not previously been done. I was releasing from within what God had put in me to be done and seen. I was now living in my realm of increase and as a result, I was constantly being positioned to be a greater blessing to others. Happiness and fulfillment were oozing forth, and real peace was felt. Contentment and pleasure were a regular part of my life now. And I know that when you decide to refuse to die with potential unleashed, you too will begin to experience a life that is overwhelming, fulfilling, increasing, and a blessing to others greater than before. What a real joy it is to have the peace of knowing that you live daily maximizing your talents, gifts, and abilities that God gave you; and that you are doing so in the place He purposed it.

> NOTHING ON THIS EARTH IS MORE REWARDING TO YOU THAN LIVING IN THE FULLNESS OF WHAT YOU ARE CAPABLE OF DOING.

Nothing on this earth is more rewarding to you than living in the _fullness_ of what you are capable of doing. You have the potential to be more, to do more, to have more, and to bless others with more. The reason it has not happened yet, is more than likely related to the truth that you haven't been challenged beyond mediocrity. The majority of the population will not go beyond comfort. And comfort will definitely rob you of fulfillment.

I'll deal with that more in the next unit. But just think: what is it that you desire to do? What is it that you are talented to do and not doing? What is it that you believe you can do, but lack confidence to do it? What is it that you have failed to do because someone else said you couldn't and you believed them? Most importantly, what is it that your Creator has ordained for you to do and you are not doing it? Do you know? The time is now! Picking up this book and reading it has been your first step towards a destiny that can be mind-blowing! Do you believe now, that you are created for more? Do you believe now that if you do not make some decisions right now, that you will take your potential to the grave? Arise! Step up, step out, and step into your new season of productivity! Release your untapped potential! You can do it, and you shall do it! Your abilities, gifts, and talents are God given and they have the God approval to be ALL that He has made them to be.

DIVISION II

Defeating the Spirit of Procrastination

NOTES

One of the greatest enemies you will ever confront is the enemy of *PROCRASTINATION*. It is the enemy that works from the inside-out, versus the ones that work from the outside-in; with the main purpose of thwarting what is on the inside. There are multiple reasons why people procrastinate. I have heard many excuses over the years about why a thing was not done. I myself have used excuses in the past, some were legitimate, and many were not. Most of the time we have convinced ourselves that our reasons, or excuses are good enough for us to NOT do more or be greater. So then, your biggest enemy is YOU! I am a firm believer that if you are going to excel and be more than mediocre; you must learn to become an *EXCUSE ELIMINATOR*. Defeating the spirit of procrastination will not be an easy task, especially if you have been catering to it for some years. But the disciplining process has to start somewhere. I am urging you to begin to apply it <u>NOW!</u> There is a scripture in Proverbs 18:9 that says: *"he also that is slothful in his work is brother to him that is a great waster."* The word *slothful* means to *be slack in doing, to forsake, be idle, leave off, and to fail.* This describes those that are lying in their graves today that did not release their full potential. And this describes those of you right now reading this book that have allowed the spirit of procrastination to take up residence in your life. Up until now, you have done one or more of the above definitions of slothful. You have either been *slack in doing, forsook to do, been idle and didn't do, or just failed to do!* How many times in the past have you used the terms: *"I'll do it later,"* or *"I'm going to get to it,"* or *"let me get back with you on that,"* or *"one of these days."* And that list can go on! Get my drift? And guess what? You never got back with them on THAT! One of these days has not yet ARRIVED! Later has continued to be just that, LATER! And you still haven't gotten around to it YET! And you are still waiting for one of these days to COME!

I remember back in the late 80's when I started building a storage unit in my back yard. I was very excited when I started on it! I got it about eighty percent finished, and it took me almost another ten years to complete it. I got it to where it was usable, but was not complete. My wife would often ask me: "Honey, when are you going to finish the building?" And my answer was just like yours: "I'm going to get to it one day soon."

Yeah, right! One day soon turned out to be a few years later before I literally became ashamed of myself. There I was—a Pastor, teacher, trainer, counselor, and community leader; yet I was *PROCRASTINATING!* It finally hit me, and when it did, it hit me hard. I was not living up to what I was telling others to do! That made me a hypocrite in that area of my life. And I was determined that I was not going to be a hypocrite any longer! That reality made me address the spirit of procrastination that was hindering me from doing more than what I was capable of. Also, it prevented me from presenting to those in my community that there was more to my life than what they could see. I was moving forward in my new life/career, but I was still allowing slothfulness to be a part of my life. This was hindering me from releasing more potential out of me. Regardless of how much you have done, or how far you have come, there is still more that can be achieved. As long as you allow yourself to entertain the spirit of procrastination, you will not have a continuous flow of your potential. You see, your potential is just like an oil well that has an unending supply. As long as you are tapped into it, it will keep yielding the substance

> I WAS NOT LIVING UP TO WHAT I WAS TELLING OTHERS TO DO! THAT MADE ME A HYPOCRITE IN THAT AREA OF MY LIFE.

you need to accomplish more! But the minute you cap it, it ceases to produce. Your potential is the same, and procrastination will cause you to cap off your potential!

You have to deal with procrastination daily. Every morning you awaken, you must face yourself in the mirror and remind yourself that today will not be a slothful day! Remind yourself that you will not *fail* to do what you need or should do. You will not be slack in progressing forward with your assignment for the day. You will not permit time to be wasted today. You have to tell yourself that you will not be idle today in doing what you know needs to get done. If you become keenly aware of the time you have on this earth, you will have the desire and the will to put procrastination to flight. I discovered in the scriptures in Ephesians 5:15-16 that there were instructions given to me by my Creator. It said: *"see then that ye walk circumspectly, not as fools, but as wise, redeeming the time, because the days are evil."* This was an awakening! For me to make full use of what God had made me to be, and gifted me to do, required acknowledging and understanding the time that He had allotted me in this earth. It is a one time shot, and procrastination must be defeated! You have to stay on top of it every day in order to keep your potential flowing. You must understand, just like you are your biggest enemy, you are also your biggest motivator! No one is going to push you towards your dreams and goals harder than you! If you do not remove procrastination from your life, your motivation will lose its steam! The easiest thing to do is to drift backwards! The hardest thing to do is to stay on your "A" game! It is so true, that there have been many days in my life when I felt like letting procrastination have its way; but there was a desire within me that was stronger than the spirit of procrastination. It was a desire to honor God with my life and to be a bigger blessing to others. I wanted to set the right example, not only to those whom I serve, but most importantly, to my wife and children. And, because of that, I was able to keep myself motivated to keep potential flowing out. I knew that I had overcome that spirit, but I also knew that I had to stay on top of my "A" game or it would creep right back in. As you get older, you have the propensity to regress back into habits that were once broken and discarded from your life. Habits that hindered you at one time before, like procrastination. Therefore, based upon your current age, you may have to fight harder than someone else to stay focused on utilizing your time wisely and properly!

No one has ever achieved their dreams or goals without first addressing the spirit of procrastination.

Defeating it will be difficult, so you have to go in with a made-up mind that you are not going to take your God-given talents, gifts, and abilities to the grave. But, you will arise and become extraordinary in your life! It must now become a fixture in your mind that: "YOU ARE MORE THAN A CONQUEROR!" A new attitude for a new life has to surface! Whatever the reasons have been before, they cannot be tolerated now. The spirit of procrastination has to be told that, "ITS DEFEAT IS NOT OPTIONAL!" Refuse to allow it to linger any longer in your presence! This is your very moment to take charge of your actions and your life. You have the potential to be greater and to do more. Do not allow laziness or slothfulness to be a part of your living. This is the time to be determined to separate who God has made you to be from who you have permitted yourself to be. Procrastination has denied you access into a fulfilling life that leads to a rewarding destiny. One of procrastinations' greatest assets is stopping you from entering the doors of opportunity at an appointed time. Great achievements have *"open windows"* of opportunity, and when you procrastinate you miss that window. You need to ask yourself

> THIS IS YOUR VERY MOMENT TO TAKE CHARGE OF YOUR ACTIONS AND YOUR LIFE. YOU HAVE THE POTENTIAL TO BE GREATER AND TO DO MORE.

the tough question: "how many times will I get to do this based upon the time allotted me on this earth?" Realizing that time waits for no man should be enough to make you rise and proceed forward in doing what you have neglected to do for too long. To truly defeat the spirit of procrastination, you will definitely have to remove some things from your life, and re-organize your daily routines. As a ministry leader and worker's trainer, I once taught on the topic of *DISCIPLINE*. In doing so, I broke the word discipline down and expounded on each letter. Whereas, I will not give out all of this information in this book, I will give you what the "D" stands for. It is for *decisions*. You see, I was dealing with becoming empowered in life, and in order to become empowered, I had to first become disciplined. Your discipline process starts with the decisions you make right now. To remove procrastination from your life, you must make some better decisions *NOW* than you made in the past. Some of those decisions must be to remove some unnecessary things from your life, and reorganize your daily routines. Priorities must become the order of the day! Your untapped potential is waiting for you to better prioritize your life. This is what procrastination does not want you to do. The day that you decide that you will step out, step up, and step into your future making better use of what God has equipped you with, is the day that procrastination leaves your life. Waking up every morning doing what puts a smile on your face and brings joy to the heart of God is the most exciting and invigorating experience in life!

I strongly encourage you to stop procrastinating for whatever reason(s) you have used in the past. Maybe you have allowed people to cause you to procrastinate, and in the next section, I will address the wrong people syndrome. But right now, it is pertinent to your future that you no longer sanction the operation of procrastination in your life! I want you to take that first step right now towards no longer tolerating idleness, laziness, or slothfulness to exist in your presence! *Release, Remove, and Resolve!* Release from your mind any thought that says this is too hard, or attempts to hold you in delay mode. Remove from your life everything that restricts you from excelling and establishing your life at a greater level, and in an expanded dimension. Lastly, resolve in your heart and mind once and for all that there is more to you than what you have done, and that there is more to obtain in this life than what you have obtained. Distinguish between taking the time to relax, rejuvenate, and to re-invigorate your life; than just being plain lazy or procrastinating! There is a clear distinction, and you must keep that in mind. But, do not cross lanes with this! It is easy to get lazy and call it relaxing. Keep your focus on the difference so that you can make full use of your talents, gifts, and abilities. I want you to awake each day with a confession emanating from your mouth. That confession is this: *"today, I will embrace it with thanksgiving, I will do what I am suppose to do, I will enjoy doing it, and I will do it with everything that is within me."* By doing this, you are denying the spirit of procrastination from re-entering your life. You see, words are powerful, and when they are spoken with conviction, they establish in the atmosphere of your life the authority that is required for the particular situation at hand. In this case, the situation is to remove and keep away the spirit of procrastination! Developing *new habits* in your life and putting them to practice each day, is going to establish your disciplined lifestyle that may have been lacking before. Whatever your reasons in the past have been that has caused you to procrastinate, I hope that by now, you are willing to put them behind you and move forward. You have to make

> WORDS ARE POWERFUL, AND WHEN THEY ARE SPOKEN WITH CONVICTION, THEY ESTABLISH IN THE ATMOSPHERE OF YOUR LIFE THE AUTHORITY THAT IS REQUIRED FOR THE PARTICULAR SITUATION AT HAND.

decisions every day—so why not make the ones that will release your potential and usher you into a new era of life experiences? It all begins the moment you make the decision not to procrastinate any longer! Free yourself from the arduous task of trying to pursue dreams, or complete goals without dealing with first priorities. Taking the initiative to eliminate procrastination first, is the first step to easing the burden of struggling to achieve. Do not permit anything to exist any longer in your life that is not necessary to fulfilling your God-given assignment on this earth! I both encourage and admonish you to do as I did concerning that storage shed. Take a good look at what you are allowing to go undone, and decide that you will not look at that situation in that condition any longer! Stop *PROCRASTINATING!* Take action today! There is much more within you that cannot be birthed out of you until you rise up and remove far from your life that spirit of procrastination. Refuse to die and leave your potential un-offered to the world. You are more...you have more....and you can do more! But it is only if and when you stop using excuses as an escape goat for tolerating procrastination! Kill it off today! It only happens when you make it happen. So open your mouth and say out loud: "Today I choose to rid my life of laziness, slothfulness, excuses, and most of all, the spirit of procrastination! Congratulations! You are on your way to not taking your potential to the grave.

DIVISION III

―――――――――― ❧ ――――――――――

Release Yourself From Dream Blockers

NOTES

What are dream blockers? Simply put, they are people that are sent your way to block you, or to hinder you from doing what you should be doing! Failure to recognize these people will cause you to take to the grave all of your potential. What is so amazing about these people is that most of them are people who are close to your life, or that appear to be for you. This is the deception aspect of these people. They have the perception that they really do care and that they are pulling for you to succeed in life. Those are the first line of people. I'll get back to these people shortly. But then there are those who are sent your way to distract you, and to shift your focus in a new direction. These are the ones that appear in your life for a short season, but long enough to disrupt your plans and in some cases cause you to discard them altogether. At this point, your potential becomes abandoned! And when you abandon something, it is very hard to recapture it. Because as you already know, once you shift your focus, it is difficult to go back and pick up where you left off. For most of us, we just keep going in life and never go back and revisit that dream or that goal again. And this is exactly what Satan, the Devil, wants you to do! Abandon your God-given talents, gifts, and abilities! Never use them to their fullness! Never honor God with them! Never be happy, fulfilled, overwhelmed, and never bless others any more than you already have! So what is one of Satan's greatest tools? It is people! Understand this... in order to be truly effective...the people used to block your dreams and leave your potential untapped, have to be in and around your life! They have to

FOR MOST OF US, WE JUST KEEP GOING IN LIFE AND NEVER GO BACK AND REVISIT THAT DREAM OR THAT GOAL AGAIN.

have some kind of relationship with you. They have to be able to persuade you, and/or get into your thought life. And the best way to do that is to have an acquaintance with you. That is the most effective way! Now, back to the first mentions. These are usually family members, close co-workers, so called friends, and those in your social and religious network. This is why it can be very difficult to detect dream blockers. It is because they are people that you think or believe you can trust, and that are rooting for you to excel in life. But oh boy, that is not the case most of the time! Now there is a real shocker!

There is also something called *jealousy*. And this

spirit can be devastating to your potential. In the scriptures, there was such a case. It was between a King named Saul, and a shepherd boy named David. In the book of 1st Samuel, chapter 18:1-9, there is story of Saul's jealousy towards David's ability to be a greater soldier than himself. In verses 7-9 we can see this *dream blockers'* perception of David, and his attitude towards David shifted once David began to release his abilities, gifts, and talents in a greater measure. It reads: *"and the women answered one another as they played, and said, Saul hath slain his thousands, and David his ten thousands. And Saul was very wroth (angry), and the saying displeased him; and he said, they have ascribed unto David ten thousands, and to me they have ascribed but thousands: and what can he have more but the kingdom? And Saul eyed David from that day and forward."* This is a prime example of others around you not wanting you to exceed or excel beyond where they are. And the very moment they see you becoming capable, or demonstrating talents, gifts, and/or abilities that is greater than theirs, they become jealous. The process of denying you goes into motion. Whatever they can do to kill-off your vision, goals, and dreams, they will do. They begin to plot (as such was the case with king Saul) to stop you from progressing any further in life. In some instances it is clearly seen, but in other instances their tactics are camouflaged. It is because of the "sin nature" that man was born with, that we live in a society where there is an adage that says: *"it is a dog-eat-dog world we live in."* What this really means is that, no one wants to see anyone else achieve in life more than him or herself. And when it appears that you can do greater than them, become bigger than them, and do more than them, they seek to get rid of you any way they can. They are dream blockers and potential killers! <u>And the best way to detect them is to watch what they are not doing to assist you in your efforts to release your full potential.</u> I will speak more on this in another section. But you have to be alert to these people, and you must be willing to separate yourself from them. It does not matter who they are to you, and this sometimes can be very painful and emotional. But if you are going to be used in this life by your Creator to do more, have more, and bless more, it is vital that you release these people from your immediate presence. I have learned over the years of my life to do what I call: *"loving people from a distance."* This means that I recognize that they are not rooting for me to maximize my potential, and that they will block my dreams and hinder me from reaching my goals. As a result, I have to separate myself from them.

Some of them were family members, and that can hurt real deep. But I had a stronger desire to share with this world what God had put in me. I was determined to change a generational lifestyle, and to present to my generation a greater image than the one before me. Because of that, I was able to let go and move forward. If I had allowed my attachment to them to be stronger than my desire to honor God and release out of me what he had equipped me with, I would not be writing this book! And many other things that I have been able to accomplish would never have been done. Some of you right now, are struggling with this very problem! You have family and long time acquaintances that seem hard for you to say *NO* to! But if you don't shake off these dream blockers now, they will keep you living in mediocrity. And mediocrity was not meant for you! You have more to offer, and there is more to you than what you have previously done. Jesus Christ said something very potent in the scriptures when he said this in Matthew 12:30: *"he that is not with me is against me; and he that gathereth not with me scattereth abroad."* This is a simple, yet very powerful statement! Even

> DREAM BLOCKERS ARE DESIGNED BY YOUR ENEMY (SATAN) TO BE IN YOUR LIFE SO THAT YOU WILL NOT BE ENCOURAGED TO MOVE BEYOND YOUR CIRCLE OF NORMALCY.

Christ says that you need to recognize who is for you in this life, and who is against you in this life. Who is going to bless you in your efforts, and who is going to hinder you in your efforts? That becomes your question to answer. Dream blockers are designed by your enemy (Satan) to be in your life so that you will not be encouraged to move beyond your circle of normalcy. It is in normalcy that you take your potential to the grave! Begin to discern those around you right now! Don't misunderstand me, I did not say begin to look at everybody in your life with a suspicious eye! Discern means to be able to read the intent, attitude, conduct, and demeanor of the people that are daily in your life and see if they truly are pulling for you. Once you listen more than you talk, you will be able to get a clearer picture of these people. It is in quietness that your senses become sharper! What comes out of people's mouths will always tell you what is in their hearts. Eventually they will speak their mind, just give them time and space! The real individual will show up. You can only pretend for so long. But you can not detect the real individual if you do not shift your stance towards life. This requires that you change your approach towards them so that you can better see their true motives towards you. Ulterior motives are always hidden, and only revealed when your wisdom becomes greater than the one with the motive. I refuse to allow a dream blocker to linger in my presence. I have entered into another dimension in my wisdom, where I am immediately asking myself the question every time I meet new people: "why are we talking?" In other words, what is the purpose behind my time being given to this person? If it is not aiding my cause, then why am I wasting my time? This is NOT a selfish thing, rather it is a wise thing! You have to be able to do what I call: "DISCERN YOUR TRAVEL." Discerning your travel is detecting what spirit is trying to operate in your atmosphere of life! Is it here to block me, or to help me? Is this person here to distract me from releasing my potential? Is this person in my life to discourage me? What are they saying when we are together? Listen more than you speak, and you will be able to perceive their true intentions. Dream blockers are usually negative in their conversation. They usually have enough excuses to last a lifetime with them. They take pleasure in seeing you "under-achieve." And lastly, they seem to find ways not to do more. WOW! Are you now starting to recognize anyone in your life like this? They could very possibly be your dream blocker! Discreetly remove yourself from their presence. Never permit anyone that is not for you to have fellowship with you. They plot to stop you! They are either a present *dream-killer*, or they will become a future *dream-killer.* You have too much at stake to tolerate people in your life that will not promote you. Your life is too short on this earth to allow those that are speaking negative towards your potential to exist in your presence! Today is the day that you release them from their Satanic assignment! Why do I call it a Satanic assignment? Simply because, as I stated earlier, they are either *"for you, or against you."* And if they are not urging you to achieve more and be more, then they obviously are not for you! That makes their purpose for connecting to you an ungodly thing! Anything that is not promoting God's agenda for your life, is definitely promoting God's adversary, the Devil's agenda! You can still be nice to people that are not for you, or that are your dream-blocker. Just because you are able to discern them now, and you release them from your company, does not mean that you develop an attitude against them and treat them cruel. Disconnect without resentment. Not only is it the right way to disconnect, but it will keep your heart and mind at peace and in the right spirit with your Creator. To say the least, it is a hard

> YOUR LIFE IS TOO SHORT ON THIS EARTH TO ALLOW THOSE THAT ARE SPEAKING NEGATIVE TOWARDS YOUR POTENTIAL TO EXIST IN YOUR PRESENCE!

thing to do sometimes, especially when they are kinfolk, as well as those that may have been called 'friend' for a while. Once you detect and discern their true purpose, you may find out that the disconnect can be somewhat strenuous to you mentally. But it is of great necessity if you are going to unlock, unleash, and live in your full potential! Remember, that dream-blockers are satisfied being mediocre, and they want those that are in their circle of influence to be just like them. The moment you begin to take initiative and start releasing your un-tapped potential, is the very moment that you will begin to expose them for who they really are to you! They are everyone from a parent, to a superior on your job, and all in between! They come in all colors, shapes, and with various IQ's. They are from elite societies as well as low status regions of society.

In other words, dream-blockers do not have any specific background status. They are just that, dream-blockers! Their mission, as I alluded to earlier, is to stop you from ascribing to be the best you were created to be, and from utilizing and maximizing your full God-given potential! The sooner you recognize them and discon-nect from them, the quicker you can excel in what you have desired to do and what you were envisioning for your life. Your next level of living is awaiting! The dream-blocker must go NOW! You don't have time to procrastinate or delay! Everyday, and every minute of your day is precious time! And the sooner you take advantage of your time and release your full potential, the sooner you can realize your dreams and goals for your life. Today is the day that dream-blockers receive their eviction notice from your life! Say it out loud...NO MORE...NO MORE...NO MORE TOLERATING ANYONE THAT WILL NOT SUPPORT ME IN RELEASING MY FULL POTENTIAL! Sorry dream-blocker...but today, you must go! I have too much at stake for you to deny me to accomplish! I am refusing to allow you to block me any longer from releasing my full potential! I love you, but you can not stay in my life any longer! As you begin to excel and move away from how it used to be, your dream blockers will begin to drift further and further away from your life. Recognize them, and eliminate them! Your future is greater than their presence! And if you know that their presence in your life is not a benefit to your life, then it is time for them to exit. You will realize later that the decision you made to rid them was one of the greatest decisions you have ever made! Your potential to achieve your goals and fulfill your dreams is greater than any personal relationship or so called friendship that does not support you. Remove the dream-blockers so that potential can be realized! Or keep them in place, and take your potential to the grave. The choice is yours, but I must say, choose wisely, time is short.

DIVISION IV

Refusing the "NO" Answer

NOTES

It is probably one of the most discouraging things, if not the most discouraging thing that anyone can hear; and that is, the word "NO." The "no" answer comes from every direction you travel, and can come sometimes from the mouths of those whom you least expect. I want to address the "no" answer from two different perspectives so that you will understand that there is a "no" that you need to accept! But the "no" answer in this section is one that you need to refuse! There will be times when "no" is a good thing. It is in those times that the Lord of your purpose is navigating your destiny on your behalf. Sometimes in this life we have the tendency to be anxious and it is in those times that we make mistakes in our decision-making process. It is in those times that our heavenly Father will block some things *for* us. That is the time when you will hear a *no* answer that may anger you. It is because you may not see any technical or logical reason why you are hearing no! I recall a time when I was going to buy a house that the church owned. The church was in a financial dilemma and I was going to purchase the property to help. It appeared to be a win-win situation for both me and the church. I could get the house for a very good price, and the proceeds would help the church out of their financial problem. It appeared that I would be tapping into my potential to create prosperity at another level for my family and my future. I was attempting to do something that I had never done before, and that was to become an Investment Property Manager, or an Investor in Real Estate. Yes! I was taking my talent, gift, and ability to create wealth to another level! Sounds good right? But God saw something that I did not see. He saw further ahead, further down the road of life than I was capable of seeing. You see, my credit score was 749 at the time. My asset to debt ratio was very good at the time. My financial status was okay at the time. And when I applied for the loan, they found one tiny little glitch that was very explainable and very understandable. But it prohibited me from obtaining a mortgage for that house from several different lending agencies. I got upset with the company that I was working with because I could not understand why they were unable to obtain a loan on my behalf. If anyone qualified for an Investment loan, surely I did! After several weeks of dealings, I cancelled the application. The church sold the property a few weeks later and we were able to rectify our problem. But now the property was gone from the church, and could not be repurchased for church use in the future. You see, my plans was to sell it back later at the market value of that particular time. Surely the church and myself would have made out okay. Again, it appeared to be a future win-win situation. But the Lord saw that my soon coming future was going to be sacked with problems that would have prohibited me from paying that monthly mortgage. A year and a half later, I was hit with medical bills that were difficult to manage. My wife's health began to decline, and it was then that the Holy Spirit spoke to me and said: "that deal you got upset about...I blocked it." I immediately began to thank the Lord for stopping that deal from going through. Had God not said "NO" to me at that time, I would have been in some very deep trouble later! That was a "no" that saved my life! At the time, I was so caught-up in what I was trying to do, that I was not focusing on what the Lord was trying to save me from. I was blinded by the fact that I was releasing my potential to accomplish more in life, and at the time, it felt good.

But in the midst of doing something that was of a good nature and of a good intent, I was going to hurt myself later in a worse way! This is the "no" that you must learn to accept and be thankful for. It is the "no" that will help you and not hurt you. Now that you understand this "no," let me talk to you now about the "no" that you should refuse to hear. It is the answer that is sent from Satan and is intended to abort your process and progress. It is designed to make you so discouraged, that you abandon your efforts to release the untapped potential inside of your spirit. *No* can be a devastating response when you have committed yourself fervently towards excelling. All of a sudden, you hear the word "NO," and it can make you stop dead in your tracks. It is not what you were expecting to hear, and definitely not what you want to hear! There is a vast amount of the population in our society that have given up on their dreams, their visions, and their goals in life simply because they heard "NO." And that no that they heard caused them to quit. This is the reason I spoke to you earlier about disciplining yourself. If you are not discipline-minded, your will to fight will not be strong enough to override the no that you heard. Before I continue, let me clarify what I mean by the "no" answer. The "no" answer is *anything or anyone that attempts to hinder, impede, delay, or deny* you from releasing your full potential. It comes from people as well as from occurrences. You have to be particularly alert to occurrences because it is through occurrences that Satan is tactful in his efforts to keep you from functioning in your full potential. Through people, he develops situations and circumstances that attempt to demand your time. This is known as a *"Focus Shift."* The situation or circumstance is designed to take your attention away from where it should be. This is a sly effort to deny you from tapping into your potential. It is designed to keep you from taking the righteous and proper advantage of your time. And

THE SITUATION OR CIRCUMSTANCE IS DESIGNED TO TAKE YOUR ATTENTION AWAY FROM WHERE IT SHOULD BE.

probably the most devastating of all, it is designed to literally make you abort any previous decisions or plans that you had made concerning excelling beyond where you are currently. Wherein, these situations may appear to be legitimate in nature, they have an underlying cause that does not pertain to what you are trying to accomplish. Two particular scriptures come to mind that shed some light on what I am talking about. One is in Luke 9:59-62 where Jesus addresses this kind of ordeal. It says: *"and he said unto another, follow me. But*

*he said, Lord, suffer me first to go and bury my father.
Jesus said unto him, let the dead bury their dead, but go
thy and preach the kingdom of God. And another also
said, Lord, I will follow thee, but let me first do bid them
farewell which are at home in my house. And Jesus said
unto him, no man, having put his hand to the plough, and
looking back, is fit for the kingdom of God."* Now, let me
help you to understand the message that is given here.
Many people will look at this and not see the Jesus that
they have heard taught to them in their Sunday School
classes. This does not sound like the Jesus of love, does
it? But it is! This is the Jesus that is dealing with developing and maintaining the right focus in every situation. Because if you don't, then your previous confession, and your previous efforts become null and void.
The dead burying their dead speaks towards those that
were not followers of him, burying those that were literally dead. But in both of these scenarios Jesus is addressing *priorities and commitment.* It is not that he was
being cruel towards understanding each man's situation, rather he was attempting to get them to be focused
on what they had said they were going to do, and that
was to follow him. The major point here that I want to
draft from this and convey to you, is that you can not
allow certain situations and circumstances to stop you

from moving forward in what you said you were going to do: regardless of how legitimate or reasonable they appear! And this is exactly the point that Jesus was making. Either you are going to take care of my business was the message, or you are going to always allow other matters to distract you and delay you. His message was to them: *"what and where are your priorities?" What and where are your commitments? Who are you more loyal to, me or that problem?* You see, the message was about maintaining a proper perspective even in the face of reasonable and legitimate circumstances. Those situations and circumstances are what I call the four *Ds* that ultimately cause your potential to go to the grave. Those circumstances and situations are there to Distract, Deter, Delay, and Deny you from entering into the place of your dreams, your goals, and your fullest potential in this life! They are your "NO" answers in the form of problems! For most of us, we have never looked at it this way before! This is something brand new to us, a truly new revelation on life! There are times in the past where you have given your attention and time to issues like this, and it has taken you completely away from what you were doing, or said you would do, prior to it. The sad thing is, you never returned to what you were doing! Or you never started what you said you would do! That no answer in the form of a matter in life, took you out of, and away from what you had going on beforehand. Know this, that just like Jesus informed the man with the dead parent that there was someone for that problem, but it was not him; so it is in every area of life. There is someone else that can handle that situation, and you are not them! Never think that if you don't stop what you are doing and get involved, that it will not be attended to! It will! You need to stay focused on what you have said you would do, and on letting

NEVER THINK THAT IF YOU DON'T STOP WHAT YOU ARE DOING AND GET INVOLVED, THAT IT WILL NOT BE ATTENDED TO! IT WILL!

your potential that is yearning to be released take place! As bad as your flesh may desire to get involved, you have to maintain proper focus to what you need to do, versus what you may want to do. The other aspect that you need to understand about these types of problems is that others will try to make you feel guilty if you don't get involved. Satan will use people to bring a *"guilt trip"* to your mind. For example: "it is family reunion time, but you are in the middle of ascertaining to a greater and more productive life. You know that if you don't handle certain critical steps in the plan right now, that you will miss a critical deadline for a major move to take place.

And taking this time out to attend a reunion with some people that haven't been in touch with you for years, doesn't make for good sound wisdom. Yet, there are some that will ridicule you and attempt to make you feel guilty for not showing up." Here is the thing...you can choose to have a couple of days of family mingling time with many that really don't care much about you anyway, or you can stay committed to the task at hand that you know needs your right now attention! The choice will be made based upon your focus on *prioritizing and commitment.* This is the time for you to show the kind of discipline that is required in order to release potential. Again, your flesh will always desire to take you in the opposite direction of your dreams, vision, or goals! You have to recognize what is happening and be willing to refuse this type of "NO" answer that is opposing your plans. I have termed this: *"THE PEOPLE PROBLEM NO ANSWER."* Your refusal to cater to it qualifies you to obtain more and to do more. Do not think for one moment that this will make you popular among the ordinaries, it won't. Prepare to be criticized and shunned by many. But what you will accomplish in this life that you had not previously accomplished, has a far greater reward than the criticism that you will experience. The other "NO" answer comes by way of what I call: *"THE*

MATERIAL PROBLEM NO ANSWER." In 1st Samuel chapter 30, a man by the name of David is confronted with a situation that would probably cause the most disciplined-minded person to throw in the towel and give up. It is a situation that says with the loudest of voices..."you can not do it...you can not go any further... this is it!" He has been out in a war zone fighting with his army of men, and he comes back home to find that his city has been raided and all of his family and finances have been taken away. Also the family and finances of his men were gone. Another army had swooped in while he was preoccupied with another battle, and depleted his living status. You and I both realize that without resources of some nature, you can not survive. And you and I know that when everything you have has been taken away from you, that it is extremely hard to focus on anything else at the time. In this 30th chapter, it says in verse 4: *"then David and the people that were with him lifted up their voice and wept, until they had no more power to weep."* This was a defining moment for David's life! This situation, without question was there to deny him his elevation to become King of Israel. It was there to stop him from releasing his full potential in life. There was more to him than being a fighter and war strategist. He had a King in him that had to manifest.

This problem was there to check his focus and commitment. In verse 6 it says: *"and David was greatly distressed, for the people spake of stoning him...but David encouraged himself in the Lord his God."* When you hear and see this kind of "no" answer in your life, this is one of the first things that you have to do. You must immediately <u>ENCOURAGE</u> *yourself!* You must stay focused on what you have to accomplish. David had to occupy the King's Throne, and this set-back, or temporary delay was not going to stop him from getting there! You can't allow it to stop you from getting there. That is the place of releasing more, doing more, obtaining more, and blessing more! You are going to have these kinds of situations occur in life, but regardless of how dire or disastrous they are, you have to maintain a clear head and a right focus, even when everyone else around you seems to be losing theirs! The result of David not acting like the others, and encouraging himself in God's purpose for his life, enabled him to pray (or consult with God) about the material problem that was at hand. In verse 8 it says: *"and David enquired at the Lord, saying, should I pursue after this troop? Shall I overtake them? And he answered him, Pursue: for thou shalt surely overtake them, and without fail recover all."* What a powerful answer the Lord gave David concerning this matter! Allow me to paraphrase this! He says to David, get up, get yourself together, this is not the end! Go after these men and reclaim what is yours! Get your belongings back! And get on with your goals towards occupying the King's Throne! Do you see this? God was letting David know that this "no" answer that you just received in the form of a material and financial problem; shall not stop you from releasing your full God-given potential. Allow me now to say this. Whatever you may be experiencing in this area, or may experience, do not permit it to dictate to you your course of action! You dictate to it the course of action that you know is required to take in order to release your potential and to obtain your goals! The power to move forward and to accomplish is still in your possession. You can not sit in the cesspool of self pity and brood over a temporary loss! Encourage yourself when no one else is around to do so, or when no one else will do so! You can do it, and you must do it! You can not afford to let that answer of "no" shut you down. Your purpose in life, and the fact that you desire to fulfill it is enough to propel you forward in the midst of hard trials. The truth that you desire to maximize your potential is enough to motivate you to get up from this minor set-back and go full speed ahead! These two particular areas of "NO" are disguised to thwart your purpose and make you abandon your dreams. You have to learn to discern them when they arise and defeat them on the spot. Do not permit them to have free reign in your life. Yes, they are very challenging, and they can be very taxing on you both mentally and emotionally. But you must remain vigilant on what you have set out to do. And you must be determined to not take your potential to the grave! Now that you have a better understanding of these two types of "no" answers, let me talk to you some more about the people "no" answers. That is, those that flat out deny you verbally, or that reject you when you are proceeding for-

> YOU HAVE TO LEARN TO DIS-CERN THEM WHEN THEY ARISE AND DEFEAT THEM ON THE SPOT.

ward with your plans to maximize your potential. These "no" answers are the least of your concerns, or at least they should be. Why? Because they are powerless to stop you! The most they can do is test your "passion-stamina." That is, your ability to persevere. These "no" responses can make you begin to question yourself. They can make you start to ponder and wonder whether you should really be doing this or not. And that is exactly what they are ultimately designed to do, make you doubt yourself! Once you start doubting yourself, your will to persevere will begin to diminish. Your desire to keep pushing when the efforts seem to be futile will fade. Enough "no" responses can have you changing your mind about what you are doing, if you do not have an absolute resolve that you are doing the right thing in the right season of your life. Perseverance is the order of the day when people verbally deny you! Having your vision fixed straight ahead and not on the denials is how you ought to be marching! I am living proof that if you keep-on-keeping-on regardless of who says no, that it will pay-off for you in the end! In my life, I have had door after door to be slammed in my face, as the saying goes; yet I was persuaded in my heart and mind that what I was doing was right, and in the right season. And because of it, I had a determination that was second to none! It was a *"will to fulfill"* that kept me pressing on in spite of the denials that I was receiving! And I want to strongly encourage you to have a determination to press beyond every "no" response that you receive. Because there will be that one "yes" answer that you have been waiting to hear that will come at the end! You can not permit those that oppose you to negatively impact your desire to release your full potential! As David encouraged himself, you too, will have to constantly remind and reaffirm yourself that you are headed in the right direction. People are going to deny you, reject you, and refuse you; but you have to know that there is that one and right someone that will say yes. I will talk more about that in the next unit. So then, "no" can be a good thing! It can be your motivation along the way to releasing your full potential. It can be a real self-testing factor to see if you are determined to be greater, do more, and bless more! Do not despise the "no" answer nor those that give it. Rather, allow it to develop within you a more positive attitude about life, and towards people. Understand that it really does take a composite of challenges in life to bring out of you either the very best, or the very worst. You decide which one you will allow those challenges to bring forth. As for me, they have, and they still do bring out the very best that God has predestined for my life! I have learned to hear a "no" response and not be moved by it any longer. I smile and move on to the next one. And you can do the same. I heard a great man of God say once: "you don't need everybody liking you, just the right somebody liking you." Refuse the "NO" answer! Do not allow it to stop your momentum in releasing your full potential. Make it your driving force that catapults you from the place you stand now, to the place you see yourself standing! When those that you think should say yes, say no, take that deep breath, smile, and move to the next one. Sometimes, you will have to take a step back and make sure that the "no" you heard was not the result of being improperly prepared. In other words, you may have to reanalyze and reevaluate what you are doing. Remember that the "no" answer is a good thing! Everyone that says no to you is not always opposing you, and this is the flip side of being denied that you need to be aware of. There may be a time that you are refused, rejected, and denied because you are not as ready as you may think to enter into the next phase of what you are trying to achieve. This is the time to revisit your project, whatever it may be. Sometimes you will have to go back to the drawing table and look at what you need to improve on in order to ascertain that you are on the right path, and in the right season or time. This is even more so a reason why you need to adhere to the "no" answer and not be distraught. There is always something positive to take away with you when you hear "no." Sure, sometimes it is the opposition working against you; but sometimes it is for your own good. Remember my story about the house I was trying to buy? That "no" that I received worked for my good! And I am so thankful today that I heard "NO"

> UNDERSTAND THAT IT REALLY DOES TAKE A COMPOSITE OF CHALLENGES IN LIFE TO BRING OUT OF YOU EITHER THE VERY BEST, OR THE VERY WORST.

when I wanted to hear yes! Therefore, pursue your vision, your dream, and your goals to be more, have more, and to give more in life with the mindset that "no" is not a bad thing for me. Go on, make the move you need to make right now that will release the potential that is within you! You have heard "no" before and it stopped you. But this time, you are using it as a motivator! This time, you have a better perspective on why you are hearing "no!" And this time around, you are using it to push harder, and to release your untapped potential! Go on, you can do it! Dismiss the image of "NO" from your mind. Yes, you are more than a conqueror! And yes you can do what many others have said was impossible for you. No is not a bad thing. Use it to excel and be the greatest that you were created to bc in what you were talented and gifted to do.

DIVISION V

Discerning Assistants

NOTES

We have reached the finale of this wonderful book. And I must say, I hope the information in this book has challenged you, inspired you, and most importantly, empowered you. There is so much more to your life than what you have seen thus far, and no matter what you have been through, you still have time to release your potential. You are a walking, living, and breathing power-house of a creature. And you are talented and gifted to do greater works in this earth before you leave it! That brings me to the purpose for this portion of this book. And that is, that there are people out here in our society that are assigned to assist you with your vision, dream, and/or goals. I call these people: "potential assistants." They enter your life to assist you in releasing your talents and gifts in their fullest ability. But the problem that many have is that they have become so affected by the "dream blockers" and/or "NO" answers that they fail to recognize their assistants! If you have never had someone to mentor you, or someone that knows how to guide you through these times in your life; then you may not know how to recognize your help when it arrives. You become so guarded against people because of what you experienced negatively, that you fail to realize what is now at your disposal positively. Have you ever found yourself resisting the good because of the impact the bad had on you? Well, I have! And let me tell you, it can be a permanent abortion of your potential if you don't have the will to persevere, and the mental perspective or the reality that all people are not the same! There are those that, their purpose for this time of your life is to assist you with what you are doing. One of the unique things about the creation of humanity is that, God designed it so that we are helpers of one another. Therefore, there will always be someone out there that has an assignment from God to assist you in releasing your potential! You have the responsibility of detecting them. And the worst thing that you can do, is to become so obsessed with your season of trial and error, that you dismiss your assistants from your life prematurely! WOW! Now that you are motivated to tap into your potential, start to focus on those that are in your life, and the reason they are there. As long as you are on this planet, people are going to enter

> THERE ARE THOSE THAT, THEIR PURPOSE FOR THIS TIME OF YOUR LIFE IS TO ASSIST YOU WITH WHAT YOU ARE DOING.

your life, and people are going to exit your life. But you have to make sure that you know why they came, more so than why they left! Yes sir, it is most important that you recognize and acknowledge your assistants so that they can help you unleash that powerful potential that is resting on the inside of you. One of the key factors in recognizing those that are assigned to help you is that they have what you need for the time, to assist you. Whether it is talent, information, or resources, they are willing to aide you with it, and they do so with gladness. These assistants seem to appear, or arrive on the scene at the time when it appears that no one cares, or when you have exhausted all measures. God has a way of allowing the right people, at the right time, to enter your life when you have the desire and perseverance to pursue and overcome! What you need to make sure of is that you will not *"take your potential"* to your grave! Those assigned to assist you with your next step, your next phase, or your next level, can not come to you if you have given up on yourself. Knowing that God has someone waiting in the wings of your life to help you become all that you were created to be, is within itself a great motivator. And because you are determined to leave this world having made full use of all your talents, gifts, and abilities, you will always have more assistants than you will *"dream-blockers."* Those that come to assist you will require the minimum from you, if anything at all. You see, many times, while they are giving you what you need, they are also receiving what they need, either from you, or from another source. This is one of the unique things about the cycle of life. Even when there are those that are takers only, there are also exchangers among us! What do I mean by that? Simply this, that our society has more people that will aide and assist one another, than it has of those that just take away.

Now that I have covered that aspect of those assigned to assist you, allow me to elaborate in more detail about your assistants and their season assigned. When you are *Desirous, Determined, and Disciplined* in making full use of the life you have been given, you will always encounter what I call *"lifers"* and *"passer-by"* people. The lifers are there for the long haul, and the passer-by is there for a season. Sometimes that season is short, and sometimes it is long; regardless of the length, it is still seasonal. Armed with this insight, you can now discern the difference between those that will be an extension of you and to you, versus those that are there to give you what you need for the moment. Never expect seasonal assistants to be loyal and dedicated to your vision or goal. They are only there to give you what you need for that vision or goal, based upon the step, phase, or level that you are in. They will be faithful and committed for the time that they are to assist you. And when they have given you all that you need from them for that time, they will separate from you. Know the difference between your lifers and your passer-by people. Your lifers will always be loyal, committed, and dedicated to your vision or goal even when they don't always have what you need at the moment to advance your potential. Yet, they always have your concern at heart, and they are always poised to do what they can to help the seasonal people in your life. Your lifers will protect your best interest at all times, the passerby won't. They are not there for that purpose. I, personally, have in the past, confused the two. And as a result, I have suffered setbacks in fulfilling or achieving the goal that I was working towards. I have since learned to distinguish the difference. I have here at my Church on our visitors cards an adage that says: *"Never try to implement a life vision with a passerby. It will cause you a life long frustration!"* You see, those that are assigned to assist you for a sea-

> YOUR LIFERS WILL PROTECT YOUR BEST INTEREST AT ALL TIMES, THE PASSERBY WON'T. THEY ARE NOT THERE FOR THAT PURPOSE.

son, will never fully understand your overall vision, or even care much at all about your goals. They are only there to give you a piece of what you need for the time. That time can be three weeks, three months, or three years. But when that time is up, they are gone. There have been too many Pastors that have grown weary and frustrated in their calling because they confused the two types of people that entered their ministry to help. You share your vision with lifers, but you share your present place in that vision with the passerby! I felt like quitting on my calling to ministry because of this. I became very frustrated trying to get temporary people to receive and understand what was meant for permanent people. I hope you are understanding and receiving this information. It will help you to proceed forward with releasing your potential to do bigger, better, and greater things before you die. This is true for secular corporations, small businesses, or for those that desire to accomplish personal tasks and missions in life. Your long term, or lifers, can not always release unto you what you need at a particular time, or at a particular place in the process. This is where you have to recognize those that enter into your life for the season you are in. They come to give to you at the moment, what the lifers don't have. They are the gap-fillers so to speak. I am speaking to you mostly from a Pastorate or a corporate leadership position, but I have discovered that this perspective is true in life generally, regardless of what position you hold in life. Once you have this understanding, you are able to move forward with your vision and goal. You know how to not dismiss your assistants that are coming to aide you in releasing all of your potential. You also understand their presence with you, and you know how to handle them, or deal with them as a result. I have another saying that says: *"Discern your travel... know why someone has entered your atmosphere...or why you have been privileged to enter someone else's atmosphere."* I believe that it is either for the purpose of me assisting them, them assisting me, or both parties assisting each other. In other words, they have something to deposit into me, I have something to deposit into them, or it is mutual. I don't believe life is lived in coincidence, happenstance, or what some call luck. I believe that life is lived, or should be lived in *"divine design."* That means that everything that I am about in life should have a divine purpose attached to it. For those of you reading this, and you believe that you were created by an almighty God with divine purpose, then you have to discern your travel through this earth. You need to begin to become more aware of your day-to-day movement. Attempting to fulfill a vision, or attain a particular goal in life, will mean that you tap into the talent, gift, or ability within you. And that will require the knowledge or the insight as to why someone has entered your space. Are they there to help you, receive from you, or both? Remember, we have already covered the *"dream-blockers"* and the "NO" people. So we understand now that we literally need to discern the entire composite of purpose and potential. But right now I am addressing those sent to assist you with releasing your potential. So then, it is vital that you recognize these people that will enter your life to help you fulfill your dreams, accomplish your goals, and excel your vision. They

...IT IS IMPOR-
TANT THAT YOU
UNDERSTAND
WHY [PEOPLE] ARE
ENTERING YOUR
LIFE AT A PARTIC-
ULAR SEASON.

are on assignment themselves, and the time they have with you is just as critical to them as it is to you! Remember I said earlier, they enter your life at the time of your need in order that you may achieve your mission. But in many instances, they are also releasing their potential in the process. That is, they are releasing more of their talents, gifts, and abilities while they assist you. So it is important that you understand why they are entering your life at a particular season. It is amazing how God has orchestrated our lives and how things work when we follow his will and his plans for us. Receive those that are willing to aid you in life. Your full potential will not manifest without the assistance of others in this world. Someone, somewhere, is assigned to help you. And someone, somewhere is assigned to help them. The cycle of aiding and assisting is continuous when you are willing to reveal and expose the potential that is within you. Think about it, we have covered a lot concerning *"potential,"* and you now have a lot to consider before you die. The question now becomes: *"will you rise up and seize the moment?"* Someone is awaiting your next move! They can not and will not enter your life until you decide to tap into your potential! People are watching you every day, waiting to see what you will do next. It is up to you to show them what is contained on the inside that you are about to reveal. You have the talent, you have the gift, and you have the ability to do what has been floating through your mind for years. You can do what you talked about in the past, but have yet to act on. You can achieve it, conquer it, and obtain it! But there has to be a will, a desire, a motivation that goes beyond the obstacles. The drive on the inside has to be stronger than the problems that will arise. You can do it! There is more of you, and more to you! Never, ever, allow anyone or anything to hinder your forward motion, stop your dreams, block your vision, or deny you access to greater! There are people that will assist you, and they are waiting for you to unleash the ability to perform the task. Remember why you were created, what you were created for, and the purpose that your Creator has for you. Keep your focus clear, your mind fixed on what is necessary, and your will yielded to fulfill your life's mission! *POTENTIAL* is waiting to come forth and reveal the blessing that has been prepared for you before the foundation of the world. You have the talent! You have the gift! You have the ability! And the only one that can stop that from coming forth is YOU! God has designed humankind with these features and qualities. And when a man or woman makes up his or her mind to do a thing, the possibilities become unlimited! Stop looking backwards on what did or didn't happen in the past; THAT'S OVER! Stop holding on to thoughts that some *dream blocker,* or some _NO_ person spoke to you in the past! Release yourself from the hurt and the pain of yesterday, and allow the God of creation to bring healing into your heart! Forgive those that have wronged you! Forgive yourself for past failures! Receive right now the healing and the anointing that will catapult you into your future! You have the potential to be greater, do greater, and to have greater! No one can take that away from you if you are willing to proceed forward in your purpose. Your help is nigh unto you. Things are closer to becoming a reality than you think. It is not as difficult to do as it may have appeared in the past. Stop complicating the simplicities! Take that deep breath, exhale, rise up, and enter in to the life that is more fulfilling! It would be a denial to the generation behind you if you died without leaving all that you have to offer this world, behind you! Uncap, tap into, and unleash your potential! Show those that are watching from a distance that you are capable and able to make dreams come true; visions for life to manifest, and that you can obtain your goal! Do not, I repeat, do not take your *"potential"* to the grave! There is too much at stake for you to die without releasing all that God has given you to do. Too many lives depend on what you have to offer. Lives that you might not ever meet, but the results of what you do will have a major impact in places that are waiting to receive the fruits of your labor. As we come to the closing of this powerful and insightful piece of information, I want you to start declaring out loud every day that: *"THERE IS NOTHING IMPOSSIBLE FOR ME BECAUSE I BELIEVE IN MY HEART THAT GOD HAS EQUIPPED ME WITH TALENTS, GIFTS, AND ABILITIES THAT ENABLE ME TO DO*

GREAT THINGS!" Declare out loud that: *"I REFUSE TO LEAVE THIS WORLD BEFORE I RELEASE ALL OF THE POTENTIAL THAT IS WITHIN ME!"* You will, because you can! Your assistants are on standby, and they will aid you in the areas of need. Life in all of its fullness is still, YET BUT A MOMENT IN TIME! In other words, it is short and brief in comparison to eternity. Thus, you should awaken each day ready to live your life fulfilling your divine purpose. Arise from your sleep each morning with the desire to face the day yielding to the potential within you to do greater, achieve greater, and bless others greater than the day before. Challenges, circumstances, trials, and tests of life will rear their heads; but you must maintain your focus to bring the vision to pass and to ascertain the goal set. You have the potential to change the course of not only your life, but the lives of those that are connected to you. Remember the definition of potential, and that is: *"existing in possibility, and capable of development into actuality."* You are currently existing in *"divine possibilities"* and you have the *"divine talents, gifts, and abilities"* to make it a tangible entity. Manifestation of what you have thought about can be seen! You have the *"POTENTIAL"* to do what has not yet been done! I urge you, and encourage you, to decide right now, if you haven't already, that you will not, *"TAKE YOUR POTENTIAL TO THE GRAVE."* The next time you ride by a grave yard, think of how many bodies that could be laying in it that did not live their lives to their fullest potential. Then I want you to think about how many graveyards there are world wide and multiply that number. I realize that you and I do not have the numbers, but I just wanted to provoke your thinking concerning those that died without making possibilities, actualities. Millions upon millions that never lived their lives to the maximum potential are in those graves! Many reasons and excuses are lying in those graves! Do not allow that to be you! Do not live so that

DO NOT LIVE SO THAT YOUR HEAD STONE CAN ONLY READ THIS WAY: "HERE LIES POTENTIAL"

your head stone can only read this way: *"HERE LIES POTENTIAL."* If no one else has ever told you before, I tell you now, you can do it, and there are those in our society who are waiting to help you. Your life is not over, rather, it is just beginning to reveal to the world around it what has been laying dormant, and put on hold, for far too long. Today is your day that you will arise and begin to unlock, uncap, and tap into your potential! Because you will not die and take *YOUR POTENTIAL TO THE GRAVE!"*

WISDOM POWER NUGGETS

Notes

These *Wisdom Power Nuggets* are for your daily motivation to move you toward making an indelible mark in the earth on behalf of the kingdom. Wise application to known truth yields the desired results in your life! So heed to these words of wisdom and watch your life soar to new and greater dimensions of fulfillment.

"THE ONLY IMPOSSIBLE THING...IS THAT WHICH YOU HAVE FAILED TO BELIEVE...AND THAT WHICH GOD DID NOT DECLARE!"

"NEVER ALLOW SUBSTITUTES TO OCCUPY YOUR PLANNED MOMENTS IN LIFE...THEY WILL DETER AND DEFER YOUR VISION AND GOALS."

"ASSOCIATE WITH A FOOLISH PERSON...AND YOU WILL SOON REALIZE THAT YOU HAVE ADOPTED THEIR WAYS. THE SAME IS TRUE WITH A WISE PERSON!"

"OPPORTUNITIES ARE NOT ACCIDENTALLY STUMBLED UPON...THEY ARE CREATED THROUGH PREPARATION."

"GOD ESTABLISHED TIME FOR A DIVINE PURPOSE TO BE ACHIEVED BY MAN. EVERYTHING YOU DO SHOULD BE DONE IN DIVINE TIMING! IT IS CRITICAL TO YOUR

POTENTIAL!"

"CHALLENGES WILL DETERMINE CONNECTION STATUS. IF ACCEPTED, THERE IS A HOOK-UP...IF NOT, THERE IS A SEPARATION. CHALLENGE RELATIONSHIPS."

"WITHOUT A FAILURE...SUCCESS WOULD NEVER BE REALIZED! DON'T BE AFRAID OF SUCCEEDING! GET UP...AND GO AGAIN!"

"NEVER EXPECT FREE MENTORSHIP...IT IS THE NORMAL OF HUMAN NATURE TO DEVALUE WHAT IS FREE! SOW INTO YOUR MENTORS' LIFE...YOU WILL VALUE THE INFORMATION GIVEN!"

"THE PRICE IT COSTS FOR WISDOM...IS FAR LESS THAN THE PRICE YOU PAY WHEN YOU LIVE WITHOUT IT!"

"LEARN TO UTILIZE THOSE AROUND YOU TO AID YOUR CAUSE. NEVER ALLOW LOAFERS AND LEECHES TO BE IN YOUR COMPANY!"

"REPETITION IS HABITUAL! WHATEVER YOU CONSTANTLY REPEAT...YOU CONSTANTLY MANIFEST! WHAT DO YOU WANT TO SEE? BECOME CONSTANT IN FORMING THE HABITS THAT WILL MANIFEST IT!"

"WHEN QUITTING IS NOT AN OPTION...VICTORY IS INEVITABLE!" DON'T QUIT!

BISHOP E. D. RICHARDSON

Bishop Richardson is the Founder and Pastor of New Beginning Empowerment Church in Hampton, Virginia, where he oversees numerous ministries that he and his belated wife implemented. He is the Founder and Executive Director of Intime Outreach Inc., a non-profit community development corporation, also based in Hampton, Virginia. Bishop Richardson is a member of the Council Of Bishops with the International Ministers Covenant Fellowship under the leadership of Prelate Bishop L. N. Peterson. Bishop Richardson is the author of "Beyond The Vows..".a book that deals with marriage relationships beyond the place of your vows. A very informative and enlightening book. He is a Ministry Trainer that believes in "Excellence of Execution for the Work-Of-The-Ministry." He conducts an annual Leaders and Workers Workshop, and avails himself for Ministries that are serious about having Divine Order and Ministry Excellence in their works. Bishop Richardson thrives to stay on the cutting edge of modern day ministry operations, and constantly seeks to excel in ways to reach the masses of lost souls. He has a heart to see the Church living in Divine Kingdom Order, and receiving Divine Kingdom Promises to manifest in their lives daily. His ministry assignment is expanding in this time of his life to include the continent of Africa. And he is expecting the Lord to expand it further before his time is over in this earth. He is a straight arrow shooter when it comes to delivering the Word of God, he holds nothing back. A voice that exudes the anointing! His delivery style is captivating, thought provoking, spiritually challenging, and illuminating to say the least! He has a saying that goes: "love me or leave me... you'll never forget me!" Once you hear this great man of God minister, you understand why he says this. Bishop Richardson has four adult children, and ten grandchildren. He currently resides in the city of Hampton, in the state of Virginia.

To invite Bishop Richardson for your next Conference, Workshop, Revival, or Fellowship Session, he can be reached at www.newbeginningec.com. Click on menu tab "about" and go to "Ministry Engagements." It's just that easy!